CPP

This book should be returned to any branch of the
Lancashire County Library on or before the date shown

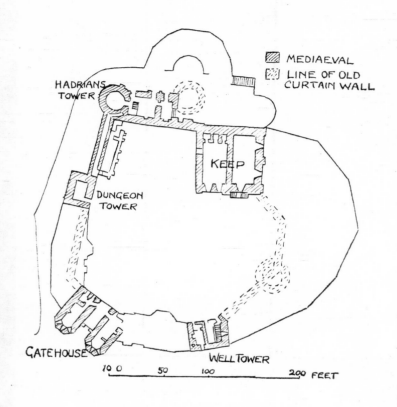

MEDIAEVAL
LINE OF OLD
CURTAIN WALL

HADRIANS TOWER

KEEP

DUNGEON TOWER

GATEHOUSE

WELL TOWER

10 0   50   100   200 FEET

Lancaster Castle

Lancashire Castles and Towers

Compiled and Illustrated

by

Leslie Irving Gibson

F.S.A. Scot.

DALESMAN BOOKS
1977

THE DALESMAN PUBLISHING COMPANY LTD.,
CLAPHAM (via Lancaster), NORTH YORKSHIRE.

First Published 1977.

© Exors. Leslie Irving Gibson, 1977.

*Cover illustration of Hornby Castle
by Bruce Danz.*

ISBN : O   85206   397   O

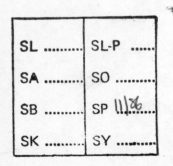
Printed in Great Britain by
GEO. TODD & SON,
Marlborough Street, Whitehaven.

CONTENTS

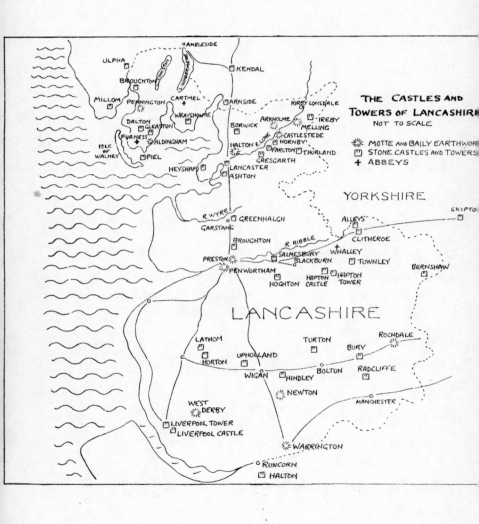

THE CASTLES AND
TOWERS OF LANCASHIRE
NOT TO SCALE

✳ MOTTE AND BAILY EARTHWORK
⌂ STONE CASTLES AND TOWERS
✝ ABBEYS

YORKSHIRE

LANCASHIRE

PREFACE

AFTER exploring and sketching castles in Scotland, Northumberland and the Lake District, the writer was surprised to find so many in Lancashire. As no book appeared to have been published covering all the known castles, towers and sites in the county, it was thought that an attempt to gather together some information on these — with some brief account of the men and their families who built and lived in them — would be of interest and also useful as a record of pieces of history which are fast disappearing. Without any doubt the list is far from complete; some not mentioned here may be well known elsewhere and remains of others whose walls and foundations are hidden underground will very probably be brought to light in the future.

The period covered here is from the time the Normans came in the 11th century and built the first true castles in this country to the 16th century. After this time, various factors such as the use of artillery, a more settled form of law and order in the country and desire for greater comfort in a dwelling place made their use and purpose unnecessary and undesirable, although some of them were strengthened and used during the Civil War in the 17th century. Unfortunately we have not many castles left in Lancashire still in their medieval state. Cromwell was probably the worst enemy of our heritage of castles, but requirement of land for other purposes has often been the reason for their destruction, even as it is today with ancient buildings. Liverpool Castle was pulled down so that a church could be built on the site and Bury Castle also made way for other buildings.

I wish to record my thanks to the staffs at the several libraries, Bury, Warrington and others, and particularly Waterloo, Liverpool, where most of my reading was done, for their willing help at all times.

INTRODUCTION

WHEN the Normans invaded England and commenced to occupy the country, William — as he had promised — divided the land among his followers. Most of Lancashire was granted to Roger de Poitou, a kinsman of William, and he in turn apportioned his domains to his knights. One of the first considerations and needs of these knights, stationed in wild and desolate country and surrounded by hostile natives many of whom had had their manors taken by the newcomers, was to find a headquarters and a home and make it safe against hostile attack without delay.

The type of castle which had been used by the Normans in Europe was eminently suited for them here. It was the motte and bailey castle which could be built quickly and be defended easily by comparatively few men. It consisted of an earthen mound (the motte) with a wooden tower on top and a flat space or court (the bailey) adjoining the motte on one side. There would be a ditch between the motte and the bailey and one surrounding them both. The earth from the ditches was used to form a rampart on the outer side of the ditch, and strong palisades of wood and thorns round the motte and bailey made a strong little fortress in the days before the long-range bow, the longbow, came into use.

The tower on the motte was the private home of the lord and was approached from the bailey by a drawbridge or a sloping flight of steps as shown in the sketch. In the event of the bailey being taken by attackers the motte would be the last stage of the defence and the steep and slippery slope of the mound was a difficult obstacle. There was no issue of commando boots in those days.

Where possible a natural mound could be used and if necessary heightened artificially. In other cases a whole mound would have to be built. At Clitheroe for example the natural limestone hill was a perfect ready-made motte requiring only the wall and tower on top, whereas at Warrington and West Derby complete mounds would have to be erected. The bailey would have wooden buildings for stables, stores, kitchens, workshops and quarters for the soldiers.

As the Anglo-Saxon chronicle tells us "the Normans built castles wide throughout the land and they oppressed the poor folk and wearied all England with their erections." During the first century of the Norman occupation there were more castles in the land than ever before or since. It was generally considered that Royal consent was required for the building of a castle but in King Stephen's time not much notice was taken of this and great numbers of "adulterine" or unlicensed castles were built. Henry II however commanded that

Typical motte and bailey castle

these castles be destroyed and it then became necessary for application to be made for a regular form of licence. He destroyed more than 1,100 of these unlicensed strongholds.

The Anglo-Saxon Chronicle also informs us that William's first act when he landed in England was to consolidate his position by building a castle even before he met Harold's army in battle, and the Bayeux Tapestry shows a picture of the building of the castle mound and tower at Hastings. This picture and a few others on the tapestry are, unfortunately, the only contemporary illustrations we have of the motte and bailey and none of the castles has survived in a complete form. Many of them were in use for a long time; in fact, the period of the timber castle in this country may be said to have covered about two hundred years because a few were built in Edward the Confessor's time before the Norman Conquest and some existed until the early part of the fourteenth century. The Earl of Lancaster burnt down the wooden castle at Wakefield in 1317.

Gradually, however, these fortifications of timber, unless they fell into disuse, were replaced by buildings of stone in this country and in Europe. There were several reasons for this change. One weakness of the wooden castle was its lack of resistance to fire and burning. The stone was far safer in this respect and gave greater strength, especially against more powerful and longer range weapons which were being made. This change of type of castle and material was just part of the long story of attack and defence which began with stones, wooden clubs, shields of wood and hide, and has continued

7

with gunpowder and tanks through to the intense efforts technically and financially for superiority in new types of weapon at the present day. The stone castle also allowed more space and comfort which was then beginning to become appreciated.

Although stone replaced timber buildings at such sites as York, Windsor, Arundel, Tamworth, Cardiff and many others, it is very interesting to note that as far as we know this did not happen anywhere in Lancashire except at Lancaster itself. When Aldingham motte and bailey became untenable because of the damage by the sea, a manor house and later a castle were built some distance away. At Clitheroe it is doubtful whether any timber building was put on the rocky mount prior to the stone tower.

Stone was also being widely used for the halls of the knights in the 14th century, especially in the north of England where the wooden halls were being constantly destroyed by fire in the Scottish raids. After the battle of Bannockburn in 1314 the Scots came to Lancaster and burnt the town and partially destroyed the castle. Again in 1322 Robert the Bruce of Scotland led a great raid and crossed Morecambe Sands from Furness. The abbey was saved from pillage by the abbot paying money to the Scots, but they burnt Lancaster again, except for the priory of the Black monks, and during the three weeks they stayed in the area destroyed Hornby, Samlesbury and other villages. All through the long period of warfare and raids when halls, houses, farms and crops were burnt it became increasingly clear that, as J. F. Curwen puts it, "the flaming brand was the chief weapon used against them."

The answer to it was a building of stone which would resist fire, and we find that the rectangular keep of a castle was the pattern of numerous "pele" towers built in the 14th century on the borders and in Yorkshire and Lancashire. The towers were three or four stories in height with vaulted basement and thick walls. A narrow winding stair in the thickness of the wall or an extension of it was a feature of the "pele." Usually a wall surrounded the tower enclosing a small courtyard for protecting the animals in times of danger.

Some of these towers such as Wraysholme and Dalton remain little altered in outside appearance except for such details as windows, and many more form part of or are the nucleus of larger halls or mansions. In Tudor times and especially in the Elizabethan era the desire for greater comfort and privacy together with the more peaceful times led to the building of mansions such as Townley, Ashton, Borwick and others.

ALDINGHAM CASTLE

THE motte and bailey castle on the shore of Morecambe Bay was the home and fortress of Michael le Fleming, kinsman of Baldwin, Earl of Flanders, when he was sent by King Rufus to take charge of the area around what is now the village of Aldingham. A Michael le Fleming is recorded as being lord of Aldingham in 1127 and it is possible that he built the castle. The mound is nearly 100 feet in height and was about 100 feet in diameter on the top giving plenty of room for a wooden tower and a surrounding palisade. About 200 yards north of the motte is a moated grange site which was very likely contemporary and used as a residence. It may have been made necessary as a dwelling because of the sea eating away the wall of the castle.

The manor of Aldingham passed to the Harringtons when Agnes, a descendant of Michael le Fleming, married Robert de Harrington, and in 1341 Sir John de Harrington had the king's licence to enclose 300 acres of his own lands, wood and marsh at Aldingham and make a park. It is almost certain that the park was at Gleaston where, prior to 1350, the family built a new castle of stone and moved there from Aldingham.

THE ALLEYS, CLITHEROE

AT the north end of the town of Clitheroe there was an ancient manor house called the Alleys, the residence of the Clyderhows and the Radcliffes. It was originally a strong tower house with a deep moat round a spacious enclosure. The Clyderhow family were mentioned in a document of 1297 when the Welsh marched through Lancashire to unite with the English in the expedition against the Scots. Richard de Radcliffe married Sybil, daughter and heiress of Robert de Clyderhow in 1322, and the Clyderhow estates passed to the Radcliffes. In 1339 Gilbert de Clyderhow and Robert de Radcliffe were served with a military summons commanding them to assemble the men at arms in Lancashire under their command and meet the king in Carlisle to repel the Scottish invader. During the same reign John de Clyderhow and Robert de Clyderhow were knights of the shire for the county of Lancashire.

The Alleys was the property of Richard Rishton of Pontalgh in 1452-3. In 1602 the estates were sold to the Heskeths of Martholme and were in the possession of the Oddies family about 1672.

ARKHOLME

OVERLOOKING the Lune and the ferry at Arkholme is a fine mound standing about a hundred feet above the river. A footpath on its north-west side follows the line of what was evidently the ditch between the mound and the bailey. As seen in the plan the church of Arkholme, which is pre-Reformation, is built with the chancel almost into the motte so the castle must have been out of use when the church was built.

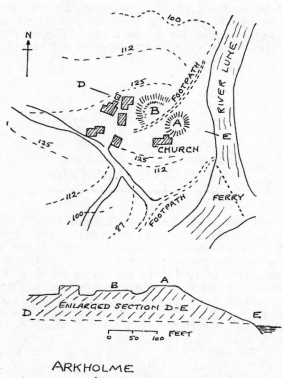

ARKHOLME
MOTTE AND BAILEY

Mr. A. White examined the motte and found a rough cobble pavement on top of the mound and another pavement about nine feet below. This was covered with charred wood, bone and bits of iron. It is probable that a Norman tower was placed on the site of an earlier British dwelling, as seems also to be the case at Penwortham, or the Normans raised the height of the mound for a second tower. A ring of flat stones found round the base of the mound was probably used as a marker ring during construction.

ASHTON HALL

THE medieval tower of Ashton Hall lies about three miles south of Lancaster overlooking the estuary of the river Lune. On its north side is the Victorian Gothic wing built in 1856. The tower, which was probably built in the late 14th century, is 57 feet east to west and 32 feet wide externally with walls 6 feet thick and 42 feet in height to the top of the battlements. At each corner is a turret, set diagonally to the main structure, 14 feet square externally and rising about 6 feet above the main wall parapet with walls nearly 4 feet thick. The parapet is embattled and carried all round the building on a corbel table. The merlons and embrasures are moulded, and the turrets have similarly corbelled battlements.

New windows have been fitted but in the basement are two embrasures of loopholes and two doorways now leading to the middle wing. The basement of the tower has a segmented barrel vault 11 feet high in the middle and 5 feet high at the sides. There was a passageway in the thickness of the wall which may have contained a stairway to the upper floors but this has now been bricked up. The tower is built of rubble masonry, mixed sandstone and gritstone, in large irregular blocks with gritstone quoins.

The manor of Ashton was part of the lands granted to Roger de Poitou by William the Norman, but after Roger was banished in 1102 the manor was held by the Lancaster family. In the time of Henry II they let half a ploughland in Ashton to Gilbert of Ashton (Eston) for a rent of one mark. Lawrence, the son of Thomas de Lancaster, had the manor and Laurence became the family name. One Laurence was made a knight in Scotland during the expedition of 1482.

On the death of John Laurence in 1514 the estates were divided among a number of families. The manor of Ashton was sold by Queen Elizabeth in 1574 to Sir Gilbert Gerard (sometime Master of the Rolls), and when he died in 1590 it passed to his descendants, the Gilberts of Bromley and the Duke of Hamilton. At the sale of the Hamilton estates in 1853 the manor of Ashton was bought by le Gendre Nicholas Starkie of Huntroyde and later passed to Mr. James

Williamson, a Lancashire manufacturer who was elevated to the peerage as Baron Ashton of Ashton. The Hall is now a golf club.

BEARNSHAW TOWER

A small turreted stone tower stood on the verge of Cliviger at the north side of Todmorden. The Lomax family had held the estate from an early period and Richard Lomax was there in 1771. The tower was standing at the end of a farmhouse until about 1860 when tradition says that it fell down when searchers for a chest of gold were digging under it. The tower is shown on a map in Dr. Whitaker's *History of Whalley*.

BORWICK HALL

THE Hall stands on rising ground about two miles east of Warton Crag overlooking the river Keer. The oldest part of the Hall is the 15th century pele tower but very little is known of its story and who built it. The manor of Borwick or Berwyk was at the time of the Norman invasion part of Earl Tostig's Beetham Lordships, and after the Conquest Roger de Poitou had it as part of his lands in the north which William the Conqueror had placed in his charge. In 1228 a Patricius de Berwyk probably had the manor, and a Ralph de Berwyk

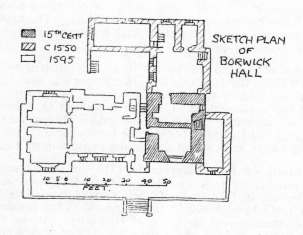

15ᵗʰ CENT
C 1550
1595

SKETCH PLAN
OF
BORWICK
HALL

10 5 0   10   20   30   40   50
FEET

Clitheroe Castle

Above : Gleaston Castle

Left : Hornby Castle

Below : Hapton Castle

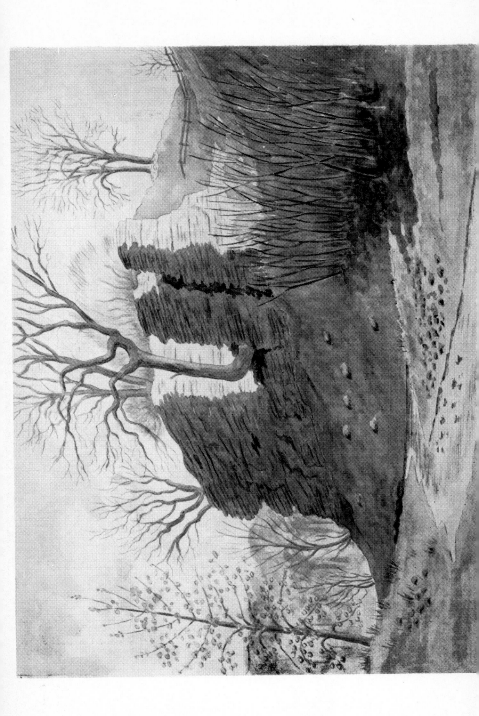

Hoghton Tower

who had land at Whittington and the manor of Berwick died in 1348. Thomas Whittington was in possession of the manor in 1489.

The Tudor and Elizabethan parts of the Hall as seen on the plan were built round the old tower which is on the right of the view of the south front. A room in the tower was used as a chapel. In a courtyard at the back of the Hall a flight of stone steps leads to a wooden verandah giving access to the upper floors.

The Hall was bought by Robert Bindloss in 1590. He was a descendant of Christopher Bindloss, a cloth dealer and alderman of Kendal in 1579. Cecilia Bindloss married a Standish and the estates of Standish and Borwick passed to the Townleys — when a later Cecilia married William Townley of Townley — and subsequently to the Stricklands of Sizergh. The Hall is now used by the Department of Education.

BROUGHTON TOWER, FURNESS

IN a park on the north side of Broughton is a mansion incorporating the 14th century tower of the Broughtons. The tower has been modernised but is in good condition with double vaulted basement, three stories and embattled parapet. The spiral stairway did connect all floors but now only links the basement and the roof. A pointed arch on the middle merlon of the parapet on the north side is carved with a shield depicting the arms of Broughton.

Sir Thomas Broughton lost his estates after joining Lambert Simnel in his unsuccessful attempt to gain the throne of England and they were granted to the Earl of Derby. After the Civil War they were sold in 1683 to Edward Leigh.

BROUGHTON TOWER

ABOUT three miles north of Preston there was a strong tower of stone surrounded by a moat fed by the Sharoe brook. We do not know when it was built but it was taken down in 1800 and a farm, Broughton Tower Farm, was erected on the site. The moat was filled in when water works were being carried out in the 1930s, and Mr. Rogerson of Broughton Tower Farm saw several large stones of the foundation of the tower and also oak posts which were in sound condition. Excavation would undoubtedly reveal the plan of the tower at least.

The manor of Broughton was part of Earl Tostig's lands before the Normans came and afterwards was held by Uctred the Saxon thegn. His family took the name of Singleton. Theobald Walter seized the manor in the time of King John but it was restored to William Singleton in 1261 by Henry III. Gilbert de Singleton was there in 1325. It was sold to the Langstons in the 16th century — Thomas Langston was wounded in a fight with the de Hoghtons in 1590 and was taken to his bed in Broughton Tower. The Rawstornes gained the estate by marriage in 1735 and, as stated above, the tower was demolished in 1800. It is interesting to note that tithes of about £20 per year are still being paid by the farmer to the church as they were when the tower was standing.

BURY CASTLE

ALTHOUGH the old English or Saxon name "Bury" indicates some form of fortification, we have no real evidence of a castle there until 1469 when Sir Thomas Pilkington had a licence to build, fortify and castellate a mansion at Bury. The first mention of Bury in documents was when Robert de Lacy made a grant of some lands there during the reign of Henry II (1154-1189).

The manor was held by the de Bury family in fief from the de Montbegons of Hornby who held lands in many counties "in capite" or direct from the king. In 1152 one Adam de Bury married Alice Montbegon and the lands were increased together with the family's importance. Another Adam de Bury was one of twelve knights appointed, in 1228, to make a perambulation of the forests in Lancashire for a survey and a report. Henry de Bury was killed at Bury in 1315 when Adam Banastre and others revolted against Thomas, Earl of Lancaster. Henry's daughter married Roger Pilkington and the estates then passed to the Pilkingtons who became a family of wealth and renown. Sir John and his son fought at Agincourt in 1415. Sir Thomas had the licence of the king Edward IV to fortify his manor at Bury in 1469. The fortunes of the family fell however after the battle of Bosworth Field in 1485, where they had supported the Yorkist cause. Their estates were confiscated and the manors of Bury and Pilkington were given to Thomas Stanley who was then created Earl of Derby for his help to the new king Henry VII. He had placed the crown on Henry's head after the battle.

During the first part of the 16th century the castle was either destroyed or allowed to decay. Leyland, the antiquary of Henry VIII, visited Bury in 1540 and wrote : "Byri on Irwell . . . . there is a ruin of a castel by the Paroch church yn the Towne." All signs of the castle vanished as the stonework above the ground was taken by the local populace for other uses and a new building was erected on the site. A ground plan of the castle remains was published in 1745 and

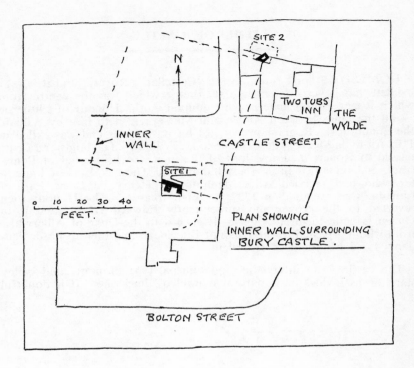

PLAN SHOWING
INNER WALL SURROUNDING
BURY CASTLE.

in 1865 part of the foundations were discovered when a sewer ditch was being dug. Excavations were made by C. Hardwick, who uncovered part of the base of a tower or keep 82 feet by 63 feet externally with walls 6 feet thick. This tower stood within a walled enclosure 120 feet by 112 feet with walls two feet thick. Another wall formed a larger court about 600 feet long east and west and 300 feet wide. The smaller enclosure was situated towards the north-east corner of this court. The map by Aitken showed how the castle was protected on the north and west sides by a steep slope and that an old branch of the river Irwell or an artificial fosse skirted the base.

In July 1973 a "dig" was organised by the Bury Archaeological group in co-operation with Bury Museum and N. Tyson's reports show confirmation of part of the earlier plan and some interesting details of the building, walls and buttresses. They also list finds of pottery dating back to the 15th century, various wood objects, parts of leather shoes, a stone cannon ball and animal bones. Further examination of the site is intended and should enable a fairly accurate plan of the castle to be made and provide valuable information and artefacts for a greater knowledge of the history of the castle at Bury.

CLITHEROE CASTLE

DOMESDAY book refers to the "Castellatus Rogeri" and it is very evident that it was the castle of Clitheroe which was the centre from which Roger Poitou governed his domain — the Honour of Clitheroe — all the lands between Ribble and Mersey given to him by William the Conqueror. Roger however lost his possessions and was exiled in 1102 for aiding Robert de Belleme in a rebellion. The lands and castle passed to Robert de Lacy, lord of the great Yorkshire fief of Pontefract, and remained in de Lacy hands until Thomas, Earl of Lancaster, who had married Alice, daughter of Henry de Lacy, Earl of Lincoln, was executed in 1322 for high treason. The Honour then reverted to the crown and subsequently Edward III granted it to Queen Isabella for life. Charles II gave it to the Duke of Albermarle from whom it passed to the Duke of Buccleugh and then to his descendants Lord Montagu of Beaulieu.

The castle is an interesting and unusual type of motte and bailey standing as it does on a natural mound of limestone. It is doubtful

CLITHEROE CASTLE

A MOUND AND TOWER
B BAILEY
C OUTER COURT

CLITHEROE CASTLE

(See also Illustration on page 13)

whether a wooden tower was ever built on the mound; the present tower of stone is attributed to Robert de Lacy, but there may have been an earlier structure. There were three floors in the present tower with entrance in the first floor and a spiral staircase in the wall at the north-west corner.

The ground floor chamber is 17 feet square with walls 8 feet thick. The buttresses against the east wall are modern and the tower is very plain. The plan shows a bailey B and an outer court C lower down than the tower. There was a chapel in the castle, the chapel of St. Michael in Castro built with the licence of the Dean of Whalley. Its position is not known but probably it was within the outer court. In common with other chantries it was destroyed during the Reformation and all trace of it has disappeared. In the de Lacy times the castle was sometimes used as a residence for the lord and at other times as a fortress, a gaol and a courthouse. The present steward's house was built in 1723.

During the raid of 1138 when the Scots attacked Furness and Craven they won a great victory over King Stephen's army at Clitheroe. It would be very interesting to know how much the castle was involved and what part it played in this battle. In 1480 Edward IV ordered it to be repaired in anticipation of border warfare. In the Civil War, Captain Cuthbert Bradkirk of Kirkham was put in command of the castle by Prince Rupert (1644) but he deserted it. After the war in 1648 the Lancaster Militia were ordered by Parliament to disarm and disband, but Colonel Assheton with 2,000 men at Clitheroe refused to do so until persuaded by Major General Lambert. The castle was then partly demolished and allowed to fall into decay.

DALTON TOWER

THE tower at Dalton was probably built in the 14th century, possibly on the site of an earlier building. It is 45 feet by 30 feet with axis north and south and is built of rubble limestone with red sandstone quoins. There were three stories as shown by corbels and doorways, and the entrance on the south-east corner was on the ground floor. Access to the stairs was originally only from the inside but an outside door was built later. The arched passage in the walls runs northwards from the stair from a doorway which is now built up. In 1545 the tower was a ruin but was repaired with material from Furness Abbey.

The manor of Dalton was held by Earl Tostig in 1066 until he was killed at Stamford Bridge, and later with other manors in the area was united to the Honour of Lancaster. Some manors were given to Michael le Fleming of Aldingham and the remainder were in 1127 given in alms for building Furness Abbey. Sometime afterwards all the manors belonged to the abbey and it may be that a castle or tower was built by an abbot of Furness probably for use as a court and prison. In the 18th century repairs were made and new windows fitted.

FARLETON CASTLE

IN his *History of Lancashire,* E. Barnes writes of Farleton near Hornby formerly held by Earl Tostig but by Roger de Poitou at Domesday, and states that it anciently had its castle and park but the castle had sunk into a state of dilapidation about 1600 and the park had disappeared entirely.

GLEASTON CASTLE

THE Harrington family at Aldingham built a new castle at Gleaston. They may have found it necessary to move from Aldingham because of the sea eating away the cliff on which their tower was built or on account of an increased number of retainers requiring more accommodation. The castle was built before 1350, probably by Sir John Harrington the Elder. It was a walled enclosure 240 feet long north and south, 120 feet wide at the south end and 150 feet wide at the north end with four corner towers. For some reason the curtain walls, although nine feet thick, were constructed of limestone rubble and were not very strong. Red sandstone dressing in the towers was some slight decoration. The keep at the north-west corner had three floors and a dungeon.

In 1415 John Harrington was granted a papal indult for a private chapel and a portable altar for mass, but it is most likely that there would have been a chapel in the castle before that date. According to one authority the castle suffered damage during the great Scottish raid of 1318. If it was existing at this time then it must have been erected before Sir John was given licence to enclose a park at Aldingham in 1341. After 1458 the castle was not occupied. Leyland noted in 1540, "there is a ruine and waulles of a castell in Lancastershire cawlyd Gleston Castell sometyme longinge to Lord Harrington now to the Marquis of Dorset." The drawing of 1727 by Buck shows the condition of the castle at that time. **(See page 14).**

Sir John de Harrington the Elder died in 1347; his grandson John succeeded and he died in 1363. His son Robert was in the king's service in France and his two sons fought at Agincourt. One, Sir John,

22

was killed, and Sir William took possession of the estate. His daughter married the son of Lord Bonville and their son, William Bonville, became Lord Harrington in 1458. Both he and his father were killed at the battle of Wakefield in 1460 fighting on the Yorkist side, and the aged Lord Bonville was executed after the Lancashire victory at St. Albans in 1461.

A grant from Robert, Abbot of St. Mary and the convent of Furness, to William Harrington, Lord of Aldingham, and Margaret his wife gave them a right of way to and from the castle of Gleaston over the Abbot's land on foot or with carriage and horses.

GREENHALGH CASTLE

THOMAS, Lord Stanley, was created Earl of Derby by Henry Tudor for his services at Bosworth in 1485. He needed protection against outlawed gentlemen whose forfeited lands had been given to him, and in 1490 obtained a licence to fortify his manor at Greenhalgh and also to enclose his park and have in it free warren and chase. Nothing is known of an earlier castle but a robbery was reported at Castlehow near Garstang in 1341. Was this Greenhalgh which is at Garstang? The Earls of Derby retained possession of the castle, except for a period after the Civil War, until 1865 when it was sold to Lord Kenlis and later to Mr. Rushton. It is now owned by Lady Cavendish-Bentinck.

The castle, standing on a small area of raised ground about 35 yards square, was rectangular with towers 24 feet square at each corner and was built of rubble and sandstone with angle quoins. The entrance was on higher ground to the east. There was probably a moat in the lower ground surrounding the castle.

Greenhalgh was one of the last two castles in Lancashire to hold out against the Parliamentary army. Lathom was the other. The Royalist garrison under Mr. Anderton the Governor "stood out stoutly all winter" when besieged by Colonel Doddington and his regiment, but on the death of Mr. Anderton they lost heart and surrendered. Timber was taken out of the building and it was left in a ruinous state. Much damage has been done by stones being taken away for building in the neighbourhood. The farm close by, Castle Farm, was built in the 17th century largely with materials from the ruin and the removal of stones still continues. Now only a small part of the western tower is left standing.

GRESGARTH HALL

ABOUT a mile south of Caton up the Arkle beck is Gresgarth Hall built on to part of a 14th century pele tower as evidenced by the walls and vaulted basement.

HALTON CASTLE

THE motte and bailey at Halton stands on the edge of a cliff about 100 yards north-east of the parish church overlooking Cole beck and the river Lune. Obviously the top of the 30 feet diameter mound is artificial. The fosse or ditch between it and the bailey is almost filled in by ploughing.

Halton was an important place before the Norman Conquest, while Lancaster was a small part of the lordship of Halton, and was held by Earl Tostig, the brother of King Harold, until he was killed at the Battle of Stamford Bridge. When the Normans came Roger de Poitou who was in charge preferred to live in Lancaster and Halton's importance decreased, although it became the centre for the chief forester of Lancashire, Roger Gernet, who held the manor in the 12th century. The Gernet family were in possession until about 1290 when Joan Gernet married William Dacre of Dacre and it stayed with the Dacres for three centuries.

In 1193 Benedict Gernet was involved in the rebellion of Count John of Mortain, but he was privileged to retain the lands and forests he held by inheritance for £20 paid for the goodwill of the king and in the following year he was deputy sheriff. There is not much known about the Dacre's interest in Lancashire. Their manor house at Halton was burnt down in a Scottish raid of 1322 and it is doubtful whether it was ever rebuilt. When the Carus family purchased the manor in 1583 they seem to have used the old rectory as their residence.

HAMPSFIELD HALL

THE site of an early pele tower is behind the 17th century Hall nearly two miles north of Cartmel. It is said that the tower was pulled down about 1850.

HAPTON CASTLE AND TOWER

ON the eastern side of Castle Clough, the deep winding gorge cut out by the stream running down the hillside from Great Hameldon to the river Calder, the castle of Hapton stood on the edge of the precipitous slopes. Nothing is known of the building of the castle, but the tower further up the hill in Hapton Park between the Old Barn and the New Barn was erected by Sir John Townley (1473-1541) and was inhabited until 1667. Dr. Whitaker spoke to two aged persons who described the ruins of the tower as they saw it in 1725. It was a large square building about six yards high and had on one side the remains of three round towers with conical bases. It appeared to have two principal entrances opposite to each other. After the Restoration the castle and the tower were in ruins and now practically nothing remains of either building above ground level. The illustration shows the of either building above ground level. The illustration **(see page 15)** shows the side of the clough on which the castle stood. The only masonry now visible is the length of wall about 12 feet long, $4\frac{1}{2}$ feet thick and about four courses high under the two trees on the top right of the picture. Very little can be seen at the site of the tower, though excavation here and at the castle would doubtless give us much more information concerning the two buildings.

The order of succession of the Hapton estates is not very clear but from the Haptons the land passed to the de Leghs (Cecilia, daughter of John de Hapton married Richard de Legh in 1205) and then to the Townleys. During the 12th century part of the manor was evidently granted to William de Arches by Robert de Lacy.

The Townley arms was probably the paternal coat of the de Leghs which their descendants continued to use after they had assumed the name of Townley after their principal residence. Sir John Townley (1473-1541) succeeded to the Townley estates at the age of nine. He was then married to his guardian's daughter, Isabella Pilkington. He served as a soldier and won a knighthood in 1497 and then settled down. Royal permission was given to him to enclose his manors of Townley and Hapton which he connected with the illegal enclosure of Horelaw at Hapton. He built the tower where he resided for long periods. He was an astute businessman, who bought corn mills, corn tithes and land and was High Sheriff of Lancashire, 1531-1541. Richard Townley, 1566-1629, in his will dated 1627 left all his armour at Whalley to his son Richard. His wife was Jane, daughter of Ralph Assheton, and her will dated 1633 in Hapton is the last instance on record of the Townleys at Hapton Tower.

HEYSHAM TOWER

E. Baines in his *History of Lancashire* says that "In Upper Heysham is a fragment of massive walling with an arch and adjoining other parts of an old wall built into a barn, the ruins of an ancient building of doubtful purpose probably one of the old border peels."

HINDLEY

A HILL in the township called Castle Hill is supposed to have been the site of a watch tower. No trace of a building remains but there were signs of a moat or trench. Hindley was a manor in the barony of Newton.

HOGHTON TOWER

THIS fine castellated stone mansion on the top of a hill 360 feet above the surrounding country was built by Thomas Hoghton in the 16th century. The older manor house of the family was probably at the foot of the hill near the river, although no remains nor records exist. One theory is that the present building replaced an earlier one in the same place but no details of the structure appear to be of earlier date than Elizabethan. The tower is approached by a long uphill drive from the road between Preston and Blackburn and has commanding views of the Welsh hills, the mountains of the Lake District and to the west the plain of Lancashire and the Irish Sea. The illustration (see page 16) shows the entrance gateway flanked by two towers and the plan shows the outer and inner courtyards. Over the archway to the inner court is a stone with the arms of Thomas de Hoghton and the much worn date 1565. Additions to the house were made in the 17th century.

Hoghton was part of the land given by William the Conqueror to Roger de Poitou, but after the latter was banished Warin Bussel held the estates. One of Warin's daughters married Hamo Pincerna or Boteler and their grandson — when he became possessed of Hoghton — took the name as his own and the family became famous in Lancashire's story. John of Gaunt granted Richard Hoghton licence to enlarge his park in the late 14th century. Alexander Hoghton was

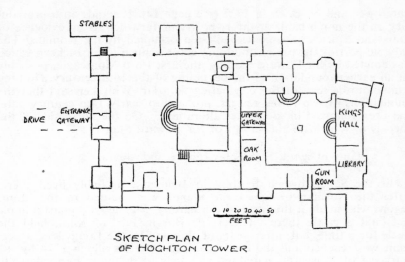

SKETCH PLAN
OF HOGHTON TOWER

made a knight in Scotland on the expedition of 1482. Thomas Hoghton who built the house in 1565 would not conform to the Protestant
faith and went to the Continent. He died in Liege in 1580 and was
buried in Douai, having been a great helper of the English Seminary
there. Thomas, a half brother who inherited later, was killed in a
family feud at Lea in 1589. His son Richard married the daughter
of Sir Gilbert Gerard. He was a High Sheriff of Lancashire, a knight
of the Shire and it was he who entertained King James I in 1617 on
the memorable occasion when James knighted "Sir Loin." Sir
Gilbert's son was an ardent Royalist, who in 1642 lit his beacon on
the top of Hoghton Tower, led the attack on Blackburn and fortified
Preston. He died in 1646 and the estate was sequestered. His son,
Sir Richard Hoghton, however, was a supporter of Cromwell and the
estate was returned to the family. In the 18th century they left the
tower to live in Walton Hall near the river Darwen and the house on
the hill became almost ruinous, but in 1862 Sir Henry de Hoghton
carried out restorations and again Hoghton was the seat of the family.

HORNBY CASTLE

THE castle at Hornby in the valley of the Lune has been the subject
of many paintings and photographs since it was rebuilt and modernised, but unfortunately we have very few pictures of it beforehand.
The illustration here is from an impression of the castle in a ruinous

state by S. and N. Buck in 1727 **(see page 14).** It stands on a promontory on the north bank of the river Wenning which, from evidence of coins and a brick pavement, had been occupied by the Romans. The only old part of the present building is the central tower or keep which was erected by Sir Edward Stanley, the first Lord Monteagle, probably on an earlier foundation at the beginning of the 16th century. Nothing remains to be seen of the original castle. Dr. Whitaker said that the foundations of two round towers, probably of early 14th century date, had been removed in some later alterations. On the north side of the keep is a stone with the motto of Sir Edward Stanley :

> Glav et' gant, E. Stanley (glaive and glove).

Ulf the Saxon owned Hornby in 1066 and probably lived there. After the Norman Conquest the manor was granted to the Montbegons who made it the head of the barony, founded a monastic home and built a castle there. Hubert de Burgh, Earl of Kent, held the castle for a time, but, after years of claiming by the Longvilers, agreement was reached and the castle passed to the Nevills in 1274 by the marriage of Margaret, daughter and heir of John de Longvilers, to Geoffrey de Nevill, a son of the Raby family. The estates belonged to the Harringtons from 1426 to 1460 when Sir Thomas and his son Sir John were both killed at the battle of Wakefield fighting for the Duke of York. Sir Thomas's daughter Anne married Sir Edward Stanley, son of the first Earl of Derby, and he received Hornby as his portion of the Harrington lordship. He was Sheriff of Lancashire for life and for his bravery at Flodden was created Lord Monteagle. He was present at the Field of the Cloth of Gold in 1520. An heiress married Edward Parker, later Lord Morley, and their son William was summoned to Parliament as Lord Monteagle. He was the peer who received the warning letter about the Gunpowder Plot.

When the Civil War came the castle was at first held for the king and many Royalists in the surrounding country took refuge there. It was besieged in 1643 and captured by Colonel Assheton but not demolished. The estates passed through several hands and were bought in 1859 by John Foster, a manufacturer from Bradford.

CASTLESTEDE, HORNBY

ONE of the finest examples in Lancashire of a motte and bailey castle is the earthwork at Castlestede about a mile north of the village of Hornby. The mound is artificial giving extensive views, and as is often the case the castle is near a river commanding or protecting the ancient ford. The main structure is well preserved with its mound, bailey ramparts and ditches. It was excavated by Dr. Lingard. No signs of any masonry were found and the site was probably abandoned when the castle at Hornby was built. The map shows the line of motte and bailey castles crossing North Lancashire along the river Lune and its tributary the Greta — Lancaster, Halton, Castlestede, Arkholme, Melling and Burton in Lonsdale.

HORTON CASTLE

IN the valley towards Lathom is a tract of country called New Park. E. Baines says that a stone building for sheltering cattle marks the place where Horton Castle once stood. It belonged to the Derbys. There is a copy of a letter in Whitaker's *History of Whalley* from Edward Derby to "my good lord the earl of Shrewsbury Lieutenant of the North" advising him of the 3,000 Lancashire men and 2,000 Cheshire men together with a list of captains in the County of Lancashire held in readiness for any invasion by the Scots." This letter is addressed from "my house at New Park 1557."

IREBY OVER HALL

THIS small village between Ingleton and Kirkby Lonsdale was the Irebi of the Domesday Survey. In 1349 Edmund de Dacre held the fourth part of one knight's fee in Ireby and Tatham from the Duke of Lancaster (see page 33). Thomas Cook, gent., lived at Ireby in the reign of James I. His family held the Hall which was known as Tottersgill or Nether Hall. The Martons also possessed it for some considerable time and were the principal landowners in the district. The initials CM with the date 1687 over the porch door are most probably those of a member of the Marton family. The illustration shows the 17th century Hall, now a farmhouse, with the very small earlier tower on the left and the Ireby beck in the foreground.

LANCASTER CASTLE

THIS is undoubtedly the best known castle in Lancashire. It stands on the west side of the town on a 120 feet high hill near the mouth of the river Lune, a strategic position on a main route between England and Scotland. The Romans realised the importance of the site and had a station here. Later there was a motte and bailey castle which in turn was replaced by one of stone, parts of which are still existing. The plan (see inside front cover) shows the mediaeval parts of the castle and the outlines of the modern additions. The dotted lines indicate the old curtain walls and flanking towers. The Norman keep known as the Lungess Tower was built by Roger de Poitou before 1102 on the mound where the original wooden tower of the motte and bailey castle had been. As mentioned in the introduction this is the only definite replacement of a motte and bailey by a stone castle on the same site known in Lancashire.

The vast estates of Roger de Poitou, "the Honour of Lancaster," were after Roger's banishment in 1102 given to Stephen who later became king. Then, when the Scots occupied Northern England, King David of Scotland possessed the castle for a few years. It is said that it was besieged and captured by the Archbishop of Canterbury during the Barons' wars against King John about the time of Magna Carta, and probably required repairs about 1209 when Ranulph de Blundeville, Earl of Chester, was Governor of the castle. He was ordered to provide men for the construction of a moat and fosses, and it is very probable that about this period Hadrian's Tower and the Dungeon Tower, the Well Tower, the curtain walls and also a gateway smaller than the present one, were built.

The castle and Honour of Lancashire were given by Henry III in 1267 to his son, Edmund, who became the first Earl of Lancaster, and the castle at this time became the seat of assizes for the county. Edmund's son, Thomas, succeeded to this earldom, and by marrying Alice de Lacy added Clitheroe, Penwortham and Halton to the estates of the house of Lancaster. His income was more than £100,000 per year, he was able to raise an army of 20,000 men and he owned the castles of Lancaster, Clitheroe, Liverpool, Halton near Widnes, Pontefract, Driffield, Tickhill, Tutbury, Kenilworth, Leicester, Norwich, Reigate and other places, but his quarrels with the king, Edward II, led to his execution at Pontefract in 1322.

In that year the Scots under Bruce made a great raid into England. They burnt Lancaster to the ground and "only the castle survived the fury"; although the Dungeon Tower and upper part of the Well Tower were badly damaged. The Scots roamed the area for nearly three weeks and destroyed the villages of Hornby, Samlesbury and other places. The town was badly burnt in 1389 when the Scots came again, but the castle proved too strong to be taken without a long siege.

Under John of Gaunt, Duke of Lancaster, the gateway was enlarged, though retaining the inner archway of the 13th century, and sometime later in the 15th century the corbelling, machicolations and the turrets were added which completed the magnificent entrance we see today. The statue of John of Gaunt was placed in a niche in the great gateway in 1822. During the reign of Queen Elizabeth, when many castles were being prepared for use in case of the expected Spanish invasion, the keep was heightened with a third storey and battlements. A stone in the battlements carries the initials of Queen Elizabeth and those of the Sheriff of Lancaster, Richard Ashton, with the date "ER 1585 RA."

Except for a few short periods, the castle has been used as a prison from the time of Henry VIII until the present time. After the Civil War, when each party in turn had held the castle and it had sustained several attacks, Parliament ordered its demolition "except for parts thereof as are necessary for the siting of the courts of justice and for the keep of the common gaol of the county." A local guide book on sale at the castle gives information regarding its use as a prison and a court of justice.

LATHOM HOUSE

IT was probably Robert Lathom who built Lathom House in the 13th century, but the manor passed into the Stanley family when Isabella Lathom married Sir John Stanley. From the legend of the Lathom foundling, Oskatel, and the tree of the eagle came the crest of the Stanleys, the eagle and child.

When Thomas, Lord Stanley, returned from the wars in France assisting Henry VII he rebuilt the house about 1496. The castle was described by Seacombe in *The House of Stanley* as standing upon a flat moorish ground encompassed by a strong wall two yards thick; upon the wall were nine towers flanking each other and in every tower were six pieces of ordnance that played three one way and three the other. Outside the wall was a moat eight yards wide and two yards deep, and on the brink of the moat between the wall and the grass was a strong row of palisades surrounding the whole. There was a high tower called the Eagle Tower in the middle of the house, and the gatehouse was also a strong and high building with a tower on each side of it. In the entrance to the first court on the top of these towers were placed the best and choicest marksmen with their fowling pieces which they levelled at the enemy, marking particularly the officers.

The story of the famous siege in 1644 and the defence by the Countess of Derby is well known, and it is a tragedy that, after the second siege in 1645 and the surrender for want of munitions, the house was slighted so effectively that no trace of it remains today.

LIVERPOOL CASTLE

THE story of Liverpool Castle is bound up with that of the motte and bailey castle at West Derby, for King John decided that the latter was not the right place for a military and administrative centre. He felt that this should be at a port, which he needed for trade and for use in his wars against Wales and Ireland. In 1207 he created Liverpool and issued a charter inviting people to come and live in the new borough "and therefore we command you that security and in our peace you come there to receive and inhabit our Burgages."

A fine stone castle was built on the highest piece of ground overlooking the river Mersey, where the statue of Queen Victoria now stands. A ditch was cut out of the solid rock surrounding the 50 yard square platform on which the castle was built. The date of commencement of building is not known but it was probably completed before 1235, when William Ferrers, Earl of Derby, was given Royal licence to "strengthen his castle at Liverpool."

There was a gatehouse with barbican at the north corner and towers at the other three corners connected by curtain walls. An interior wall divided the courtyard into two parts and a building called "the house" covered a well. The upper storey of this block was used as an armoury. The tower at the west corner was larger than the other two and was the keep. As shown on the plan by E. W. Cox, a hall and a chapel stood next to the south tower which was the residence of the lord or constable when staying in the castle. The slope of the present Lord Street was then an orchard with a dovecote between the castle and the river. In medieval times a dovecote could only be kept by a lord of the manor and even as late as 1615 we find that constables had instructions to see that this privilege was not abused.

The only remaining part of the castle to be seen is an underground passage under James Street, which originally ran from the ditch to the river. Even the Pool has disappeared.

The several drawings and plans which have been made in the past are not really satisfactory if a detailed and accurate record is required, but from bits of evidence pieced together it would seem that E. W. Cox's plan and the picture in the Picton Library based on this plan give a good impression of the castle.

When the last of the Ferrers paid with his life for supporting Simon de Montfort, the castle and of course the lordship of Lancaster and other estates in the country passed in 1267 to Henry III's son Edmund. He was created Earl of Lancaster. His son, Thomas, succeeded him and it was during his lordship that, in 1315, the castle was attacked —

Opposite : Ireby Over Hall

This page : Rochdale Castle

Opposite page : Liverpool Castle

Turton Tower

the only recorded instance before the Civil War. Adam Banastre led a revolt against Thomas, but the rising was crushed and the leaders were executed. Thomas himself was executed a few years later in 1322; he had been accused of plotting with the Scots. A year later King Edward II came to Liverpool to restore some order in the troublesome times and stayed at the castle. The roof of the hall had been repaired for his visit (cost 1s 8d) and the castle victualled. The contents of the castle according to a 14th century list included 186 pallet beds, 107 spears, 39 lances and 15 great catapults for hurling stones. Also a vat for brewing, one large and two small brass pots, one ewer with a basin for washing and a considerable amount of domestic furniture.

When John of Gaunt, Duke of Lancaster, died in 1399 the Duchy of Lancaster and the castle passed to the crown. About this time two great Lancashire families rose to power — the Stanleys and Molyneuxs who had been at Sefton since the 11th century. Both families won fame in the French Wars under Henry V and Richard Molyneux was knighted and made constable of Liverpool Castle. Later under Henry VI the Molyneuxs were made hereditary constables.

During the Civil War the castle was captured by Cromwell from the Royalists in 1647, who in the following year regained it by a night attack. The townsfolk were on the side of Parliament and several hundred of them were killed in the assault. Around 1670 the castle was partially demolished. It was garrisoned for a short time when Lord Molyneux stood for King James II and later King William used it for his operations in Ireland. The demolition in 1721 in order to free the ground for the building of St. George's Church may have been a matter for rejoicing for the people in those days, but, if the castle were standing at the top of Lord Street today, Liverpool would have a grander and more interesting piece of architecture than those she already possesses.

(See illustration on page 34 and plan on inside back cover).

THE TOWER OF LIVERPOOL

THE tower on the edge of the river Mersey near the bottom of the present Water Street was probably built about the middle of the 13th century. Sir Thomas de Lathom owned it in 1360 and after his death it passed to Sir John Stanley who had married his daughter Isabella. Sir John, the ancestor of the Earls of Derby, was a warrior famous in all Europe. He had distinguished himself in the service of Henry IV, who in 1406 gave him licence to fortify his house in Liverpool and also confirmed his lordship of the Isle of Man which Sir John had taken for himself the year before.

The tower became the fortress and town house of the Stanleys when they were not staying at their homes at Lathom and Knowsley and was a base for their journeys to and from the Isle of Man. There was, not unnaturally, rivalry between the Stanleys and the Molyneuxs of Sefton who were constables of Liverpool Castle. In 1424 there was nearly open warfare when the Molyneuxs massed their forces and prepared to attack the tower. Peace was restored however by the Sheriff without serious trouble.

In its later years the tower was not much used by the Stanleys. It housed French prisoners during the Napoleonic Wars and in 1819 was pulled down. An interesting relic was found during the demolition in the shape of a glass wine bottle of 16th century date with the eagle and child badge of the Stanleys on the neck.

MELLING

A lofty earthen mound placed on an elevated plateau about 75 feet above the marshy meadow is on the east side of the rive Lune at Melling, two miles north-east of Hornby. It has commanding views and the motte and bailey at Arkholme is about a mile away on the opposite bank of the river. The mound is in the garden of the vicarage and gardening operations have altered the base. This motte and bailey castle is one of the line of such forts across Lancashire along the rivers Lune and Greta from Lancaster to Burton in Lonsdale, just over the border in Yorkshire.

NEWTON IN MAKERFIELD

CASTLE HILL, the motte and bailey about half a mile north-east of the parish church of Newton in Makerfield, is one of the most impressive mounds in Lancashire. The extent of the bailey is not seen but the well-formed mound is a striking feature in the local scene. It is slightly oval and raised artificially on sandstone rock defended by a ditch on the north-west side and by steep slopes down to the water on the other side.

Very little is known of the history of the castle. There is mention in Domesday of a "king's house" at Newton in Edward the Confessor's time. If the castle was the king's house then it was built before the Norman Conquest. After the Conquest, Roger de Poitou, lord of the Honour of Lancaster, gave Newton to Robert Banastre and it seems reasonable to suppose that it was the home of Robert for some time.

E. Baines in his *History of Lancashire* writes of the mound as a barrow, although he did not know of any interment there. The mound was "dug" in 1843. One shaft was sunk vertically from the top and three horizontally into the sides at ground level. It was seen that clay, sand and sandstone formed the mound built on the rocky surface. A chamber 21 feet long and 2 feet square was discovered and the impression of an adult human was found on the roof of the chamber.

PENNINGTON

THE parish of Pennington lies a few miles to the south and west of Ulverston. Dr. Barber in his *Prehistoric Remains* tells us that an earthwork on an eminence known as Castle Hill is supposed to be the site of the castle of the Penningtons before the Conquest. It consists of a large circular enclosure with an entrance towards the south-east and defended on the south and east by a ditch and vallum and on the north and west by precipices.

In a field called Ellabarrow to the east of Pennington church there is a large oval mound covered with trees and known as Conynger wood, and in the adjoining field a large excavation from which the earth and stone for the mound was taken. There is a local tradition that in this mound lie the remains of Lord Ella with his golden sword beside him. On a hill just above Conynger wood is the mansion of Conynger Hurst. When this house was being rebuilt in the early 19th century a circular tomb was found and a number of bones together with an ancient sword were uncovered but they crumbled to pieces when exposed to the air.

E. Baines mentions that the manor house or castle was abandoned about 1242, and Muncaster Castle in Cumberland has been the seat of the Penningtons since that time.

Ancient rolls and registers show that Gamel de Pennington held the manor before and at the time of the Conquest. From him descended Joscelin de Penyngton who was abbot of Furness in 1181. In 1349 Alan de Penyngton held the manor of Penyngton from the abbot of Fourneys by knight's service. Later Sir John de Pennington commanded the left wing of an expedition to Scotland under the Earl of Northumberland. This Sir John gave refuge to Henry VI during the Wars of the Roses and in return the king gave him the glass cup known as the Luck of Muncaster, which the family still retain unbroken.

PENWORTHAM CASTLE

THE Domesday survey names only one castle in Lancashire in 1086, namely the motte and bailey at Penwortham. The wooden castle was built on a magnificent natural position, a hill on a ridge of land extending northwards to the edge of the south bank of the river Ribble with unimpeded views over the Fylde and to Longridge Fell. Strategically it commanded the main road north and south where it forded the river, and the steep slopes of the mound over 100 feet high with a ditch on the south side made it a very strong defensive post. On the other side of the river the ford and the road were defended by the fort at Preston.

The castle was probably erected by Roger de Poitou and after he was exiled Warins Bussel was made Baron of Penwortham. The Bussel family held the manor until it passed to the Lord of Clitheroe, Roger de Lacy, in 1205, and eventually it descended to the Earls of Lancaster and thus to the crown. It is recorded that in 1212 Thurstan Banastre held Penwortham by one "sor hawk" (a hawk in its first year). Warin Bussel's wife owned land in Evesham and he gave Penwortham church to Evesham Abbey. Three monks and a chaplain came from the monastery to perform divine services at Penwortham. At a later period the castle was held by the monks of Evesham and this may have changed the use and purpose of the castle and have possibly been a reason why, as in the case of other similar castles, it was never rebuilt in stone.

In 1856 excavations brought to light the remains of an earlier habitation of the mound, a British or Romano-British circular timber hut. There was a pavement of stone on the natural surface of the hill which was presumably the floor of the hut. Another layer of stones about five feet above this was the floor of the Norman tower. The Normans, probably without knowing, had built their wooden tower on top of the remains of the hut and about five feet of accumulated earth and debris. Several objects contemporary with the hut were found and also a prick spur of Norman type.

PIEL CASTLE

WHEN King Stephen granted all his possessions in Furness and Walney to the Abbot of Furness some fortification was constructed on the Isle of Fouldrey, a small rocky island a few acres in extent lying between the Isle of Walney and the mainland. The present stone castle was built about 1327 by Abbot John Cockerham as a defence for the abbey and a retreat for the monks during the interminable series of Scottish raids during the 14th century. The strength and size of the stronghold is an indication of the wealth of the monastic institution which built it. A broad and deep ditch on the north and west sides part the castle from the rest of the island. A curtain wall with a gatehouse at the north-east corner and three towers on the west side enclosed the inner ward, a space about 180 feet long and 150 feet wide. Any towers on the east wall and the wall itself have been washed away by the sea. The entrance was at the north-east corner direct from the sea, and the keep was in the inner ward.

King Robert the Bruce besieged the island stronghold as he ravaged Furness in 1316 during one of the great Scottish raids when the monks from the abbey were most probably taking refuge on the island. At the beginning of the 15th century however the abbot John de Bolton could not afford to maintain the castle and allowed it to fall into disrepair, although it was restored in 1429.

When the attempt to dethrone King Henry VII and make Lambert Simnel king was made, Captain Martin Swartz landed here with 7,000 German and Irish troops in 1487 and stayed the night at Swarthmoor near Ulverston before marching south to defeat by the king's forces at Stoke. Following the suppression of the monasteries, the castle was not used again, and over the years it suffered greatly from the action of the sea and many walls fell. Further damage was prevented when in 1856 the Duke of Buccleuch had protections built and made other restoration of the fabric.

PRESTON CASTLE

IN the grounds of the mansion of Tulketh at Preston there were, until about 1835, earthworks which were evidently the motte and bailey castle of the town. They were on the west side of a deep valley cut by the Moor Brook between Preston and Ashton on the southern point of a cliff 50 feet high and 80 feet above sea level. The cliff is now about 600 yards north of the bank of the river Ribble. The castle was in a strategic position for both defence and guarding the river passage with an outlook up and down the river and across to the castle at Penwortham. The two forts would guard their own side of the river and the ford which connected the important roads north and south until as late as the 18th century. The road is shown on a map of 1715. The site of the motte and bailey is now built over but the six-inch Ordnance Survey map of 1847 shows the position and shape. The mound was apparently circular, about 125 feet in diameter at the base, and the bailey was of crescent form.

The castle ceased to be used for military purposes in 1123 when Stephen, count of Boulogne, to whom it belonged, gave the site to thirteen Cistercian monks from Normandy. They stayed there for four years, and then moved to Dalton in Furness where they founded Furness Abbey on land also given to them by Stephen.

RADCLIFFE TOWER

WHAT remains of the house of one of the most important families in Lancashire stands on a level plain within a bend of the river Irwell. The red sandstone cliffs on the south side of the river gave the name to the manor. The Radcliffe lands were listed in the Domesday Survey which stated that "Rex Edward tenebat Radclive pro manerio." All the land between the Ribble and the Mersey was a royal estate of Edward the Confessor.

We do not know when the first building was erected here. In Whitaker's *History of Whalley* a pedigree of the Radcliffes of Radcliffe gives William de Radclive of Radclive Tower as one of the trusty knights of the Grand Inquest in Lancashire in 1212. The stonework we see today dates from the early 15th century. In 1403 James Radclive had licence from Henry IV to rebuild his house with crenellations and battlements. It seems from early accounts that the rebuilding consisted of two towers with a timber hall between them but nothing is known of the second tower.

The plan of the existing tower shows the five feet thick walls with a projecting plinth. The entrance is on the west side on the ground floor through a pointed arch doorway. The lower chamber was originally vaulted and has three large recesses about 10 feet wide in the north, south and east walls. They seem to have been fireplaces and the flues in the walls still remain. The sketch **(see back cover)** of the wooden hall shows the massive oak timbers and the door at the end which leads to the store tower. The hall was about 43 feet long and 27 feet wide. In the 19th century it was still being used as a hayloft and

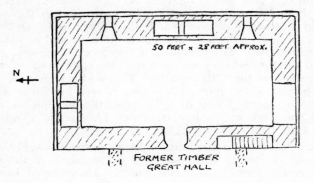

50 FEET x 28 FEET APPROX.

N

FORMER TIMBER
GREAT HALL

42

cowshed but it fell into disuse and in 1834 nothing was left except part of the tower we see today. Although one might expect a fortified house like Radcliffe to be surrounded by a moat, no trace of one has been found.

In 1529 Sir Robert Radcliffe, Lord Fitzwalter, was created Earl of Sussex. The estates were sold in 1583 to Andrew Barton of Smithhills Hall and the connection of the Radcliffe family with the tower came to an end. The hall was used by the Earl of Derby in 1592 for housing widows of recusants.

The parish church of Radcliffe is about 200 yards to the north of the tower. It has been considerably altered but the form of its arches are similar to those in the tower and the church may have been built about the same time. An alabaster slab, much worn, covered a tomb which was probably that of a grandson of James, the builder of the new tower and hall in 1403. The inscription round the edge is rubbed away except for the name Jacobi Radcliff. The knight and his lady, a Langton, are inscribed on the slab and the two shields show the arms of Radcliffe and probably Langton.

ROCHDALE CASTLE

ABOUT a quarter of a mile south-west of the parish church of Rochdale and on the west side of the Manchester road is Castle Hill, the site of a motte and bailey which must have been magnificent in its day with the Pennine hills all round and the river Roche curving round the base of the hill. In the early days the waters of the mere were a quarter of a mile to the east, and the castle overlooked the ancient ford known as Trefford. The illustration (see page 35) shows the hill from the north with the castle house on top. Very little signs of a motte and bailey are to be seen now, but part of the earth rampart surrounding the bailey (B) remains.

A few notes and a plan of the castle appear in Henry Fishwick's *History of Rochdale*. A charter of the 12th century refers to a castle of Rochdale and a deed of about 1238 mentions "land bounded on one side by the ditch of the castle." The charter shows that it stood on rising ground overlooking the valley of the river Roche. What is now Rochdale was originally entirely within the township of Castleton and the phrase "Villa Castelli de Racheham" occurs in an early 13th century charter.

As is too often the case, we do not know who built the castle or who lived there or used it, but it would be under the command of the de Lacys. At the time of the Conquest, Gamal the Saxon thegn had the land in Castleton and Rochdale and he continued to hold it afterwards. He was probably made a knight and it may be that he or his family built the castle. They owned land in Elland in Yorkshire and took the name of Elland. In 1212 a survey showed that the manor was held by a number of tenements including Hugh de Elland. The paramount lords were the de Lacys and Roger de Lacy gave the church of Rochdale to Stanlaw Abbey. The castle was important in Norman times but the wooden tower was never rebuilt in stone and was abandoned in the early 13th century. The manor passed from the Ellands to the Savilles and later to Sir John de Byron.

Mr. Page, curator of the Rochdale Museum, made an examination of the site in 1972. A trench was dug across the rampart of the bailey parallel to the line F—G, but the only finds were of 19th century pottery. The whole of the area of the bailey and mound is now covered with houses and bungalows.

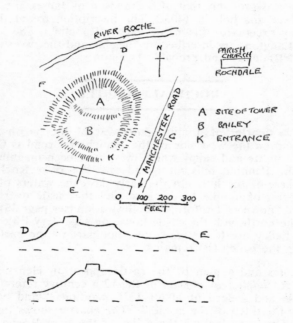

A   SITE OF TOWER
B   BAILEY
K   ENTRANCE

SAMLESBURY

THERE was a fortified house, probably a stone tower, near the river Ribble at Samlesbury in the 13th and 14th centuries. It was held by the Denyas family and was destroyed by the Scots on one of their raids into England, possibly on the great raid of 1322 when several villages in the area were ravaged. An heiress of the family,

Alicia Denyas, married Gilbert de Southworth and he built the present Samlesbury Hall in the 14th century.

THURLAND CASTLE

THE castle in the township of Cantsfield is about four miles south of Kirkby Lonsdale standing on a low mound in the flat plain with the river Greta on the south side and the Cant beck to the north. A deep circular moat surrounds the castle.

Sir Thomas Tunstall was granted a licence by Henry IV in 1402 to fortify his manor at Thurland and to make a park of 1,000 acres of meadow called Fairthwaite. He held the manor in socage of a rent of 3s 4d from John Harrington. His son, Thomas, was knighted for services at the battle of Verneuil in 1424. He married Eleanor, the widow of Philip Darcy, without the king's permission but received a pardon. Brian Tunstall, who held the castle and manor in socage as before from Lord Harrington, was killed at Flodden and his name is mentioned several times in the ballad of Flodden Field.

The manor was sold by Francis Tunstall about 1605 to Sir John Girlington. His son, Nicolas, was a strong supporter of the Royalist cause in the Civil War. He was knighted, was a major-general and was killed in 1645 at Melton Mowbray. Sir John surrendered the castle to Colonel Assheton but the Royalists recaptured it and kept it until the siege of 1643 when it was almost demolished. It had been, together with Hornby Castle, a refuge for Cavaliers during the war. Rebuilding in keeping with the old was carried out during the 19th century and there is still the appearance of a very strong fortress. There is a slit window opening in the east wing and an interesting gritstone doorway on the south side of the north wing. After passing through several hands it was bought by the Brown-Lees of Oldham. Mr. Eric Brown-Lees succeeded and was lord of the manor of Tunstall, Cantsfield and Burrow.

TOWNLEY HALL

THE present building lies just south of Burnley, and where the ground south of the Hall rises to the main Burnley-Halifax road there is a round knoll at the end of a level stretch of cultivated land. It is known as Castle Hill and was probably the first fortified site at Townley. There are indications of ditches on the eastern side. Nearby and in the township of Cliviger is a farm called the Old House, said by tradition to have been the site of an old mansion. A charter of Gilbert de la Legh is addressed "apud Clivacher" so that the mansion was probably his home, and if so it seems reasonable to think of the de la Leghs as lords of the castle.

The descendants of Geoffrey, son of the Dean of Whalley, and the daughter of Roger de Lacy had lands in Townley and took the same name. The de la Leghs became united with the Townley family when Cecilia Townley married John de la Legh and a generation or so later they assumed the name of Townley and the arms of de la Legh. It may have been John's son, Gilbert, who built the pele tower about the middle of the 14th century. This is the eastern wing of the present Townley Hall and was probably erected as a defence against Scottish raiders. The tower had walls six feet thick with corbels and machicolations but the latter have now been taken away. Additions to the tower were built and at one period they formed a quadrangle with a courtyard in the centre, but the north-east side was taken down and re-erected alongside the existing north-west wing.

One of the famous members of the Townley family was Sir John (1476-1541) who inherited the estates at the age of nine and married his guardian's daughter, Isabella Pilkington. He was knighted with the English army in Scotland. Royal permission was granted to him to make a park at Townley and at Hapton where he built the tower and lived for many years.

Townley Hall with the surrounding lands were bought by the Corporation of Burnley in 1902 and opened as a public park.

TURTON TOWER

THE tower stands about four miles north of Bolton on a picturesque stretch of moor, although Camden — when he visited it in the 16th century — found it very wild and desolate. The buildings are also picturesque. They are of three different periods, the medieval tower, the Elizabethan additions and the 19th century parts. The tower is 45 feet long and 28 feet wide with four storeys, but the top floor was added later and the 15th century tower was most probably only three floors. Like many other towers, nothing is known of its beginnings during the interesting period when it was serving its real purpose as a refuge and defence in the troublesome times of the 15th and 16th centuries.

Robert de Lathom held the manor in 1212, and it then passed to the Tarbocks and later to the Orrell family. William Orrell built the Elizabethan portions in 1596. In 1628 the Orrells sold the manor to Humphrey Chetham, the founder of Chetham hospital and library. The tower is now owned by Bolton Corporation.

(See illustration on page 36).

UP HOLLAND CASTLE

THERE was evidently a castle here when the de Hollands were the lords. Sir Robert de Holland had a licence in 1304 to fortify his mansion at Holland. He took part in the Scottish Wars at the end of the reign of Edward I and the beginning of that of Edward II. He rode in a tournament at Stepney in 1307, bearing his arms of a lion rampant on a field of fleur de lys, and as a chief justice of Chester he had charge of the royal castles of Chester, Rhuddlan and Flint.

WARRINGTON

THERE is practically nothing to be seen now of what was probably the largest motte and bailey castle in Lancashire. It covered an area of approximately three acres. The castle, situated on a low ridge, was about 100 yards north-east of the present parish church of St. Elphin and roughly 250 yards from the river Mersey. It would command the old road which crossed the river by the ford at Latchford, and it is said that it was destroyed by fire in 1260. A survey of Warrington made in 1587 described the "motte hill" as the seat of the manor or baronage now decayed. The castle was never rebuilt.

Roger de Poitou placed Paganus de Vilers in charge at Warrington, but about the end of the 12th century the lordship passed to the family of Pincerna or Boteler and, after the castle was burnt, they probably moved to Burton Wood and built Bewsey. They became known as the Botilers or Butlers of Bewsey. There was a William de Botiler at the castle who died in 1233.

The mound was excavated in 1832 and examined again when the Clergy Orphanage Schools were built on the site. It seems to have been originally a funeral mound as early pottery, bones of oxen, sheep and deer and brass ornaments were found. A well was in the hollow of the mound which had evidently been raised about nine feet, although the top three feet above the Norman paving were said to have been placed there for the Parliamentary guns besieging Warrington in 1643.

Two jet figures were also found, pieces for the game of Huaf, but it is not known where they were lying and therefore at what period they were brought to the site. Most of the finds may be seen in the museum at Warrington. A detailed account of the excavation was written by Dr. James Hendrick in 1852 (see the Historical Society of Lancashire and Cheshire papers).

WEST DERBY CASTLE

UNFORTUNATELY only very faint traces remain of the figure-of-eight moat or ditch which surrounded the once important motte and bailey castle at the Royal Manor of West Derby. It lies about 150 yards north of the church in the field still known as Castle Field on the north side of Meadow Lane. A map of Yates and Parry of 1768 shows the circular mound approximately 47 yards in diameter. The castle would probably have been built about the second half of the 11th century by Roger de Poitou who possessed it until 1102 and put William de Molines of Sefton in charge of it. During King John's struggle with the barons there was a garrison of 140 footsoldiers and 10 knights and crossbowmen. In 1197 castle repairs cost 100 shillings and between 1218 and 1225 more money was spent. Work on the drawbridge and on houses within the castle cost nearly £5 in 1227. The Earl of Derby had a warrant in 1226 for £100 per year for keeping the castles of Lancaster and West Derby.

The castle ceased to be of use when it was realised that a township on the coast with a port would be much more useful in this part of the country as a trading centre and a base for the navy. The result was the founding of the Borough of Liverpool in 1207 by King John, and the building of the castle there. The castle at West Derby evidently continued in use for a time as a writ of acquittance for expenditure on food in the Close Rolls of Henry III (1221) shows that Adam de Yeland had custody of the two royal fortresses at Lancaster and West Derby. In 1296 however the castle at West Derby was disused and in ruins.

WRAYSHOLME TOWER

THIS good example of a small pele tower stands two miles south of Cartmel near the village of Allithwaite overlooking Morecambe Bay. It was built by a branch of the Harrington family of Aldingham, probably in the 15th century — a Michael Harrington acquired a grant of freewarren in Allithwaite in 1315.

The tower is 40 feet by 28 feet with axes north and south built of local limestone rubble with angle quoins. The walls are four feet thick at the base and at the south-west corner of the tower there is a projecting garderobe about seven feet square. The original entrance was a pointed doorway at the north-west corner, and a spiral staircase on the wall at the south-west corner gave access to the upper floors.

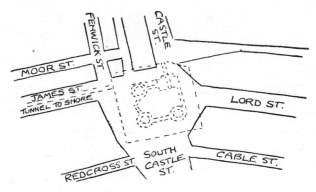

THE SITE OF LIVERPOOL CASTLE

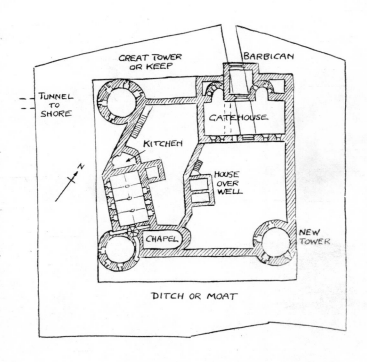

Plan of Liverpool Castle